We're Only Gonna Die....

(From Our Own Arrogance)

Hi

In this book, I oppose social-democratic accomplishments within the neoliberal regime, now being put to trial by conservative nationalism. I urge a radical way of working, cutting in our own flesh in order to sustain a critical, creative environment and urge a wolf in sheeps' clothing style of output, to engage others. I hate authority, decadence and pride.

If you'll only produce once you're fully covered. You'll produce way less and be stuck to admin work way more. A sustainable practice is in need of free or cheap labour, and consequently is tied to funding responsibilities and political stakes. Dutch right wing politicians spoke about the cultural sector's dependency on the subsidy-drip (subsidieinfuus) and they were right, this dependency turns productivity into lame government workers' efforts, stuck in bureaucracy with low result, tied to subsidy. They were not right in that cultural vitality is not a public interest and does not require subsidy. Public interest should be liberal, freethinking, independent, and not be dependent. So, me using their rhetoric of the subsidy-drip to criticise decadence in the cultural sector, kind of shows how I lack friends on all sides.

I believe independent cultural work can only foster, especially as an organisation, by generating freely available assets, and becoming financially independent. Keep it real: our democracy would not support an off-culture stimulating cultural resistance. Of course the independent sector was never given a proper chance, as discussed in this book. Nevertheless this has hardly been articulated as the 'established' sector was stuck in revisionist indexation bullshit etc.. But now, with conservative nationalism, citizenship is fully about affirmation and the sector is pretty much left to die. This book very much touches upon that.

If the purpose of true progressive work is to be resistant, they need assets without interest of others, to continue building a market independently, and complete the true mission of frustrating prevailing cultures. Cultural production as such, should not be about realising a project, but about building long term resistance. About ensuring that people can maintain their work, be productive and spark culture at large.

The current political climate will do away with all codes (fair-pay, inclusivity, governance) and will shorten the leash to NGOs on all levels possible. Especially in a technocratic environment like The Netherlands. Independence will have to be accomplished elsewhere and otherwise, and I believe I have some ideas about how I'd do that and experience of doing this. I never expressed this much, as this is not to be written in responsibilities, and was not and is still not, or hardly, acceptable to say.

I am grateful to have been able to pay myself for over 20 years while doing independent work, albeit just enough to keep me going. Perhaps I was too corrupt to be a true progressive, perhaps it was the right way to aspire being a progressive mediator.

This booklet combines several selected writings published elsewhere from 2011 to 2021–therefore spanning positions and concepts over various times–and recent notes on a whole bunch of ideas developed over time. I always positioned my work as progressive cultural production. I am stimulated by people who are into paradigm breaks, but feel I must mediate these as paradigm shifts, using design and storytelling. That is my role as editor and curator, as the proclamation and celebration of the radical in itself, in the language used there, lacks the tolerance to people outside of whatever that radical understanding is. Instead, radical stuff should be tolerant and open. I therefore hope my work effectuated radicalising work. I think it did, but that story is not included here. This book builds on these experiences and speaks to situations in abstract.

Furthermore, in the light of the rise of conservative nationalism, all positions are challenged again.

Diplomacy and therefore mediation and curating have failed, one could argue. But does this mean we should not try to be diplomats of radical work anymore and only sorrow in our own backyards as radicals on the losing end of the sad democratic hegemony? I don't think so.

I gave a lot. Maybe I gave up too much. It's difficult. Maybe it was the best way to go even if it wasn't recognised, and maybe it is the only way to be resistant in future times. The last one is an interesting matter, the first one might just be sad, but is history.

Maybe I've gotten stronger and grew vocal in my own crazy fundamentalism. Maybe too much. And maybe I just don't care about a career or conventions anymore. I am sure I felt and still feel unrecognized in a fucked-up way, but don't feel it troubles my integrity and feel clear about it. It only troubles me emotionally, but whining is not going to help, perhaps some support by speaking out more helps, but that's personal, and the private is banal: it should be about the public, like in work.

But maybe there is a fragility to this writing, perhaps it is why this booklet lacks integrity and is yet another book by a loser writing memoirs of a worthless and at times all too easy kind, being pretentious (like some of the proposals for books I receive, and fully understand). But maybe this booklet actually sparks things because it stems from lived engagement of over 20 years wherein, I don't think to have been alien, these resultant ideas went through doubt and self-doubt... but were always there and articulated. Perhaps the short no bullshit opinions hold integrity because of that. Perhaps progressive and radical people recognize themselves, can take energy out of it, or even inspiration. In an ideal scenario outsiders such as policy makers, press, educators and others in power will open and get a better idea of what it means to truly try and be progressive in the field. Maybe people will pick up the challenge to work their ass off and see where it leads, through risk and through insecurity, and take up the responsibility of progressive cultural work with a care and commitment that creates persistence to endure and sustain.

I know this book opposes many conventions, at least within the rather decadent leftist Dutch cultural landscape, and might bring fear to the safety of the equally decadent national conservative minds, in how it shows what fundamental engaged neighbours, with the same looks as any white supremist, might be willing give and bring to them do to elegantly disrupt their lives with creative appeal they'd be receptive to.

I have always embraced entrepreneurship as a safe haven. Yet, I have exploited myself tremendously if standards are to be accepted, and although ignored and abused, I have no regrets at all. Therefore, this implies I piss on those standards. I believe in productivity over self-care. I hate the decadent wellbeing state, which to me is the product of colonialism and reinforces the continuation of all its aggression. And there is so much more, where my ideas won't be appreciated much, even if it is about the consequences of these positions to the legal bodies our technocracy has built, etc. etc.. These are the matters touched upon in this book.

This writing is a statement of support to all independent progressive workers, vocal to the belief they're doing something good. I really love these people, and I hope everyone I've worked with over the years has felt at least something positive in our working relationships, of what I'm articulating and underlying and bringing together here. My mission was and is and might be even more needed now.

I feel grateful for having supported many people with deviant practices and deviant ideas over the years. They have been a great source of inspiration and motivation to me. All of them needed support in outing themselves vulnerable, and I happily provided by any means available. Perhaps this work will find support. That would be nice. This booklet is not a 'fuck you' to all others, but a reaching out, coming from a chosen precarious situation, driven by engagement.

If this writing is about anything, it is about pushing the margin to where it should be: constituting the conventional anew. Niches are for connoisseurs. I don't care about connoisseurs and niches. I care about stuff everyone should know about. Forcing stuff down throats won't work. Anger, patriarchy, supremacy doesn't work. Effort into radical love and care for cultural production has been my device. Perhaps I never cared about myself, as this was the only way to keep going, and perhaps I appeared colder from who I am at times as this has been my way for over 20 years. Evidently my heart and soul kind of lost connection there. That is the main thing I am not sure of having done well. In the end I lost too much, and perhaps some people were not able to see me for what I gave (anymore).

Sadly.

But still stuff needs to get going.

For better or for worse.

Love, Freek

So...who is this pretentious person?

Activist people might experience Freek Lomme as a populist, while popular people might extperience Freek an activist. This is exactley where he wants to be.

In the field of art, design and cultural criticism, Freek Lomme has been writing, curating, cleaning, managing directing, creative writing, artistic directing, art directing, investing, lecturing, warehouse managing, tutoring, partaking in boards and so on since 2003. Freek has been associated with various museums, independent art spaces, magazines, schools and more.

Freek founded Set Margins' publications in September 2022, after having founded and directed Onomatopee from 2006 to 2022.

As a support structure, a platform for production, a network and publisher, Set Margins' exists to frame current impulses from the margin with particular focus for communication, forms of cooperation, and involved politics. There is transparency on Set Margins' finances on the Set Margins' website.

Freek also has a modest private life including a small but rich family situation, a gender situation, a poor hobby situation and such. He used to collect things, has a wireless printer on a cable, and owns two bikes. One of his tape dispensers is wasted.

Meme by Silvio Lorusso, 2024

progressive cultural production

Progressive cultural production brings progressive ideas and experiences to mind that had not previously been considered.

It mediates between marginal and experimental cultural sensibilities and conventional cultures of the majority.
It diversifies, encourages tolerance, and stimulates curiosity and engagement.
As such it urges a liberal civil society, of informed people, of engaged people, of people with resistance to self-censorship and self-righteousness.
It stimulates creative minds and action.

Progressive cultural production enforces a dynamic culture, a living and breathing culture, where people are allowed to imagine and differ, and are welcomed in doing that. People find new ways to engage, new markets to explore, new needs to satisfy.

Progressive cultural production demands people to never be satisfied, to never stop questioning and exploring and to take responsibility for themselves first and others secondly.

Progressive cultural production urges elevation, at any level, at any time, and criticality to any authority. Only heartfelt love matches, but the heartfelt should be a lifelong challenge.

It is a fact that the music we listen to in puberty resonates most, as we open up to sounds and build our own frame of emotions along these tunes, but these should not remain.
Nostalgia in music as nostalgia at large, is a pastiche to ourselves, and a false commitment to life.*

* mind the quote at the opening of this book.... it's a song from the Bad Religions 80-85' album...so yeah: I'm an antifascist to my own believes...

On the responsability to engage in progressive cultural production.

There is responsibility to production, as production is the major objective. That is what you bring. In a precarious organization this requires very decentralized operations that require much self-organization. Nobody can micromanage. This requires an economy of trust over an economy of set standards. It also implies, more real-time, that clear communication without restraint, beyond (self)doubt, dignity and pride, is vital to get to the point, as well as tolerance to explore and fail. This can be tough or challenging depending on capacity to perform tolerance and deliver engagement.

The overall quality is to be monitored by people leading, so past failures of similar nature are taken in consideration. Proven qualities should turn into reference points and be challenged by reason to explore experiment.

Engagement can only exist based on trust, particularly in precarious organizations. Therefore, it is vital to define the commitment of engagement. How far are people willing to go giving in to the cultures of decadence western life, of paternalistic habits, of financial security and safety?

There are always possibilities to improve and deadlines to reach, which can create a pressure tank, especially when people have ambitions. It is here, again, that trust is vital to produce, and having to respect what gets done is more important than focussing on what is not realised. Nevertheless, we do learn from such experiences, and take this forward if we are tolerant to listen to needs and self-criticality.

This is to be managed explicitly, but cannot take up too much time in a precarious organization. So again: be vocal but perform beyond (self)doubt, dignity and pride without losing a sense of safety. Rigidly will feel painful and offending, as well as caring and exciting, exactly because this is what we are engaged to deliver. We cannot bullshit around and need to perform our responsibility to the product available. This means to focus on our engagement, often beyond exploitation and on the fracture of feeling exploited. There is no space for self-dignity along the paths of capitalist and colonial measures of any kind, unless it is marked by someone/anyone involved. These parameters should always be noted at the start of a project, where needs and opportunities for financial compensation, ambitions to outcome and working conditions are to be mentioned, so all involved know they are to be respected and trust is supported.

The subsequent working conditions will be defined by the support for production you establish out of the various elements of engagement by people involved, like the increasing or decreasing availability of time, the changing financial means or budget, needs for creative changes as someone proposes to kill darlings, occurring needs of post-production as nerding around might pop-up being vital to get result etc. etc.. Again: acting with persistence is vital, and trust and commitment are key. You can only make this work together, by giving and taking, by respecting what people can and cannot do. If someone performs less, is complaining all the time, draining because of lack of tolerance or simply never finishes, or if the resultant outcome did not feel right, you just don't continue with this person, or involve the person in another project that better matches their strengths. Stuff needs to work.

Often projects drain energy and capacity. Often projects will not deliver the outcome you ideally aspire, but what matters is that these projects grow less, and you will lean through experience how this will work next time you get into such a situation. Just be persistent, don't have pride or dignity and support the community.

The ability to resist stress used to be included in job descriptions but has now vanished. For good reason, as it is a repressive, paternalistic approach. Yet the ability to cope with engagement and define your position along the path is essential and a more updated, respectful version of it. It also touches upon the ability to be resistant to others and yourself, without losing the objective to deliver.

On the other end of the table, where the established bosses are situated, there must be respect for the other and hunger for what people bring out of this. As any power comes with responsibility, it is the job of the senior to suffer through this most, and fill holes where needed most, as this person will be both experienced in enduring this as conditioned by it and has the final responsibility to deliver results. This person will have to fill the gaps and put dignity and pride aside, or say no to a project, and identify additional capacity.

We do not have to evaluate and formalize processes, as there simply is no time. The work rather requires creativity and intuition supported by experience, which cannot be formalized. We just must share regrets within the informal moments in between or at times when we present the work to audiences, and finally have time to get away from performing. I explicitly call it regret, as this is what we feel. And only if internalized emotionally, we will signal the issue and perform the alternative next time: that is intuition. As such, a richer intuition is an example of self-critical vulnerability. The back end is pretty much a pressure tank all the time, as we can always work ahead if there is less urgent work to do. The front end is a façade where we pretend to follow the culture of decadence we have to subvert.

Even if work must be decentralized, there will always be overhead costs: material and expenses to cover contributors. These are often hidden costs unless you pretty much work on a project basis without any structure. This work often brings in costly people as the work is less engaged. Financial administration, cleaning, construction work, inventory management etc. are therefore precious and vital to keep the machine going. In many cases, within a precarious organization, this work will come down to the self-organizing capacity of the decentralized together. Something people don't expect and are not willing to give per se, but someone must do it. If there is no volunteer or free labor available–which is most convenient as these costs are often at disbalance with other costs and are not paid by project-funding many small places rely on– or if it simply requires professional experience, these costs may end up being compensated way better than creative work. The balance in hourly fee must be redefined in society at large. Meanwhile, this pressure on small organizations again demands them to become financially independent of subsidy to sustain. And the more formal responsibilities become, the more money will go to accountancy costs, for instance.

Self-chosen precarity for the greater good isn't easy. It defies social convention, and being on the losing end of society in a capitalist order does make one vulnerable. So, to define limits of engagement is the part in the structural change we need to build. And let's be clear: these limits are to be respected if you want to work together, but if someone else is willing to step in, the result is more relevant than the claim to credit. The claim to credit is irrelevant anyway. This is at odds with capitalist logic, but it is relevant to progressive cultural production. There is no logic to sadness when it comes to the greater good. Sadly, individual success and individual joy sells, like how people respond emotionally to stories of individual loss, grief and so on but don't always respond to actual figures and facts. That is how capitalism works and sustains, and how empathy was monetized by neoliberalism, and the reason why it got lost in conservative nationalism.

Needs of institutionalizing at the lower end of the regime

Progressive cultural production is an offer by people who want to bring tools, perspectives, experiences, information or otherwise, delivered along current events and new insights. Yet, where 'delivered along current events and new insights' has the appeal of a TEDx innovation rhetoric, or the rhetoric of neoliberal capitalism, being a wolf in sheep's clothes, the term progressive brings in another political perspective to this corporate paternalism. That is: one by voices marginalised, either social, intellectual, in merit, geographical, in means or otherwise.

Everything starts from the motivation.
The perspectives towards the conditions for operation from within the ideological margins towards increased societal support laid out in this book depart from a positioning of 'progressive cultural production'.

Such voices are precarious in their mode of operating. We all know stories of the only gay in the village. Local environments can be harsh, particularly provincial ones. The 'provincial', in its negative connotation, represents a repressive and conservative regime. This regime is a cultural environment wherein its institutions follow the merit of the majority, and therefore retain a collective consciousness that's rather conservative.

Merit feeds habit and habit creates a habitat. A habitat of collective consciousness. Institutions follow this merit in the formal structuring of legal and financial bases, and informal inclusion and exclusion, thereby sustaining a conservative habitat. They might not be aware since they invest much effort into the professional processing of this regime. This practice within this habitat is nevertheless the privilege that the power of the majority rests upon. It is also a cultural coding that includes and excludes and therefore creates an environment wherein a certain merit is rewarded and thereby sustained in conditioning by success and reward within that very habitat, which keeps a blind eye to liberal democracy itself. The majority itself, are the people who support this environment. In a democratic society, these people are the effective sovereign. When we think of democracy, we think of a liberal democracy. But the extent of the liberal in 'liberal democracy' is always to be contested, to sustain liberal democracy itself. This is evident in national and supranational issues of separation of powers, such as in debates towards the Polish and Hungarian state, or in the political bargaining of democracy for Kurds with Turkey over Nato membership hustling, and, very actual, the threat to the Dutch democracy I live in. This is our individual responsibility as sovereigns supporting liberal democracy. Yet this is often remote, particularly for the silent majority.

What it comes down to, is that a liberal democracy must remain vital by allowing liberties to the minorities which are to guard its freedoms. As is often stated: with power comes responsibility and the strong are only strong to the extent they support the weak.

Meanwhile there is power in progressive organization on a local, smaller level. Grass-root initiative is a rather futile gesture, laughed at by the capitalist regime. Likewise big chains like Media Markt advertise by promoting NO VAT discount and therefore promoting small government with means outdoing all publicity means of any local museum. Through a powerful capitalist lobby and merit by the cultural support of the sovereign, silent majority, the opportunities to embed the liberal in democracy's society are repressed. Therefore, within the capitalist regime, effective organization implies institutionalization.

Institutionalization and bureaucracy

28

The Institutional is only established as long as it is less likely to fall over, as it will take longer for all value to vanish, unless the institution does not own much and heavily depends on funding, which may be temporary. If unavoidable structural costs weigh heavy on uncertain financial grounds, institutions are financially vulnerable. If there is less commitment from the workers, if they have a 9-5 mentality, it is even more likely to lose the engaged support required to push through times of precarity. Therefore, institutions are nothing other than small spaces. Yet, if people can leave more easily, or if costs can be lowered, and if structural costs are easier to lower or cover, it is more likely for an institution to sustain. If there is some sort of value owned, they are even more healthy in resistance, since they can use that value to cover expenses: sell a work from collection, rent out a space or something. Equally there are many costs you could consider luxury: what temperature do you want in the exhibition spaces for instance.

The institutional eventually aspires to the same as a small initiative: progressive cultural production.
Yet, as the institution is bigger, engagement often decreases, as size makes people feel they have more rights. Pension, indexation etc. apply. This makes people less engaged. Workers could also invest the costs of pension into the business and create self-owned assets that help them sustain the business cooperatively instead and have a claim to result out of that.

Yet, commitment is less in a capitalist world. Many workers in institutions are less committed to the actual cultural work, but are the support structure to keep it going; financial departments, cleaners etc. PR departments are kind of stuck in the middle. Yet, there is distance by the difference of engagement between these workers and cultural workers who are more alert and engaged in the actual needs. To DIY and decentralize and self-organize this work within an institution is unthinkable...but is it?

Tuning these cultures, of different types of engagement and different needs of organizing between the different departments, often brings in bureaucracy: different forms of meetings, different formats of responsibility and briefing. It is less decentral, less self-organized, as the hats are more remote from the actual objective released by the work. While this may sound respectful and professional as it is a structure (often discussed as a model which adds time spent on this), it takes away a lot of energy. Often, instead of having meetings and evaluations you'd better just get it done yourself. Even just removing all the time spent mailing back and forth on appointments saves energy and time, as it is often the invisible hours of communicating that drain energy.

So what bureaucracy brings, both in the practice as well as in the idea of it, is something to hold on to:

a belief that we are doing things together in a smart way. A sense of professionality, a sphere of confirmation of an authority widely shared. As such, the culture of the institution tends to feed itself, and bites its own tail. It drains itself to a huge extent.
The solution is to bring trust to individual self-organization, create an environment where people can take initiative instead of being micromanaged, and are practical about things. It requires multitasking, sure, and being alert on stuff around you and things to mind. It requires experience that comes over time, and tolerance to have stuff fail.
In the institution, stuff can hardly fail. Of course, it is great when there are means available to tackle the lack of time available because of sickness or something, but often there is not, even within institutions. I'm not saying people should get lazy, but rather that we must trust people in the effort they bring and in their capacity to self-organize and express practical needs if they need more. It is up to people in charge, to allocate and keep things small. That way, most engagement with the stuff happening on the floor is generated, and most resources in terms of energy and cash are invested into the output.

Pushing

the not-for-profit

Offer is not just an opportunity of turnover, but also an opportunity of engagement and support. That is, implicitly, the liberal freedom to choose and therefore to vote for one voice over another. Key to finding support is support capacity for the marginal to release a progressive, liberal voice.

This requires infrastructure.
Infrastructure, in the neoliberal capitalist regime, is conditioned by formal regulations and cultural habitat managed by the regime.

On July 20, 2022 the news reported that major not for profits in the Netherlands paid over €2,3 million negative interest to banks, where the interest rates used to be positive on savings. They therefore requested the government to regulate, as this is absurd while going door to door for donations and knowing of the profits banks make and the bonuses they offer to stakeholders and managers.
Where these huge NGO's do lobby and have a voice, smaller legal entities pursuing alternative purposes do not.
Even more so: within the cultural sector the neoliberal habitat, which is our society, pushes cultural workers to be entrepreneurial and keep up their own pants. Yet, at the same government funding is bureaucratized by the neoliberal regime, where they require the fulfillment of certain codes in their management.

In the Netherlands, we have three codes:

1. fair practice.
This is a collective labor agreement speaking of minimum pay for freelancers and people in permanent positions.
Within a social democracy, this stems from a plan of overall regulation, matching the moral grounds of the habitat. Yet, within the neoliberal regime, this safety net isn't a social safety net, but a capitalist web to silence the marginal by institutional and legal limitations to push the counteragenda, and liberate the habitat. It is a tool to silence and keep the neoliberal capitalist habitat alive by decadent neocolonial saturation of the precariat by giving them enough to breath but not to engage, and therefore silencing them in their capacity to bring liberal democracy to practice.
Equally, where the merit of the habitat outside of state involvement by funding requirements perseveres, pushing for entrepreneurship under institutional discrimination towards liberal democracy, the marginal has little maneuvering space due to inherent lack of access to the market, banks, investors and more which are supposed to contribute to the working budgets building the marginal voice.

2. governance
The objective is to regulate authority in order to pro-

tect against misuse of power and mismanagement, and therefore to manage consistently and coherently, along processes and decision making. It does so by adding eyes to decision making processes.
The word governance stems from government. Government is a social democratic tool. Social democracy was intended to support exploited masses in a class society existing prior to the global village. Government in a social democracy would have a clear merit, intended to serve the country by a big state apparatus... would have.... At present, social democratic politics has become neoliberal, and nobody knows how to distinguish them from the former capitalists anymore. But that might change under national conservatism, where we know they are capitalist, but will not be allowed to speak out. Therefore, again, government has become a tool to repress the plural marginal. Equally, the apparatus, call it bureaucracy, is laid out as a leash technocratically operated by the neoliberal regime to silence the marginal by 'social and economic' protection along costly bureaucracy supported by jurisprudence. Particularly where free labor is a necessity, the obligation to serve this bureaucracy easily turns out leaving a no-go to organization. Furthermore, the gouvernante itself is politically urged to be someone outside of the habitat the organization is to serve, so ideally a treasurer with entry to money matters along the habitat, a corporate member as to bring in

corporate thinking, a networker with entry to stakeholders, a PR specialist and so forth all operating from within the neoliberal habitat.
This brings institutional discrimination to practice, by governing on neoliberal principles rather than ideological diversification thee not for profit is to serve.

3. diversity
This promotes equal opportunities and inclusion. Yet, given the restraints of the above this equality and inclusion can only be within the conditions of the neoliberal habitat. It excludes through merit and ideology. It stimulates for more females Magaret Thatcher style coming from privileged backgrounds, not bringing more leveling. It stimulates a repressing of slang and dialects by its merit. It unifies, rather than diversifies, and in doing so, it silences the culturally precarious by offering hope.

The meritocratic hijacking of progressive culture in neoliberal times.

Merit is never given, but should always be accomplished. Along its codes of conduct, a society based on merit is exclusive to otherness and critique. Liberal societies are taken hostage by merit, particularly where merit empathizes ethics - which is a systematic and more social determination on how to behave- over morals - which is the total of individual weightings . This is at odds with the liberal basis that a liberal society should have since it should emphasize morals.
The merit often ends up being a conduct supporting ethics which maintains conservative positions and therefore serves to moral protectionism. Where power comes with responsibility and the dignity of a society is measured by the way it copes with minorities and the deviant, we often find people within societies afraid to take on their moral, and easily start pointing by conservative ethics.

As a result we find excesses of evident institutional discrimination, but the wider currents underneath are more difficult to tackle. It is merit which sustains codes of conduct. Merit sustains its conservative culture mostly without noticing, particularly as people are not familiar with freethinking and cannot handle moral out of fear. Here self-criticism is not evident along the social ethics within group dynamics prompting moral protectionism. Merit mostly governs by unquestioned habit and by inability to understand other tongues.

Merit becomes even more fierce, once it hijacks guerilla positions: where business marketing takes over independent rhetoric, expressions and means, where placemaking and gentrification hijacks freezones, where education lacks moral schooling in social studies, where neoliberal cultural policy regulates, where institutions fail to be deviant. All such limit the possibilities of liberal society to vitalize itself.
A vital liberal society does not confirm itself out of fear, habit, protectionism and more, but contests itself by giving space and voice.

Free spaces and even safe havens are currently regulated along the lines of target groups, divided, and conquered, on the leash of the neoliberal regime. Neoliberal society plays on the feeling of social safety, where there is none. People want to contribute to something approved to be good, so they produce along the habit of a conservative authority. They receive credit for collaborating to this regime. The neoliberal plays on fears of instability and rejection. The neoliberal supports those who support it: it supports the health care of a few within its borders over the many outside of its borders which they exploit via many paths. The neoliberal promotes social respect from within these borders: borders of fear and decadence. It leaves its followers to debate tenth of percentages in salary raises, it brings them to lose themselves in insurance issues over slightly damaged bumpers (which were originally intended to bump) and so on. This is where merit became a governance of technocratic culture. All together it means that the social democratic captured within the neoliberal is used to give people a finger and take their full bodies in return. The political liberals know what they are doing, and know how to cash their profit best, where social democracy is completely forgotten. And as we speak, neoliberals are fucked over by national conservatives who only take this to yet another level.

Progressive culture is even hijacked by this rhetoric. The public sector is not to support morals that are deviant to market conformity, but to support their own agenda, and partially support the market by an incentive towards entrepreneurship. The public sector has the power to govern those without a voice with even small desks at local municipalities: one for temporary spaces or gentrification, one for placemaking, one for culture along various criteria promoting their merit and so forth: only a small price to pay for a silenced culture. Extra more so: along the 'safety-nets' they embed, they reduce capacity by the very technocratic governance that, by its' executive merit, feeds into fear and need for social safety. This merit took such deep roots in our decadent culture, that people do not just claim social safety, but even claim their wellness. This is where the ethics of liberal society corrupts tremendously. Therefore, wellbeing and wellness should be disrupted where possible. This is what marginal outsiders should do, and what the public sector in a liberal society should defend.

But who is to provide support structures for such an anarchist and humanist emancipation, true to liberal culture? Where is it expected from? Who will pay for this? Are those open to critical engagement expected to pay crazy entrance fee to 'What Design Can Do?' critical gatherings, which end up suck-up meetings amongst friends anyway? Are they expected to put their faith in Daan Roosgaarde?

No: it should start with public engagement; with the people sovereignly taking charge. It should start by engaging the un-engaged, silent majority and make them aware of their moral responsibility as human beings to themselves. Not to live in fear and hide behind protectionism, but to open to doubt and conflict and to give even knowing they will lose.
But this is a very distant situation....it's utopian thinking..
Let's start by stimulating curiosity beyond the culture of merit, maybe stimulate freethinking and understanding different tongues or dealing with different vocabularies and thereby broadening the civil range as moral practitioners. It is not up to the progressives to gather and whine. Meanwhile it surely isn't progressive to claim social rights regulated by technocra-

tic merit of the neoliberal regime. It is even more painful when progressive gathering is publicly supported as 'expert meeting' or okay for support with negligible audience engagement. It should then hit the streets forcefully, even where this is likely not to be legal or supported by public funding.

The liberal society we cherish as reality is a mirage. The liberal society we claim on Christian, Jewish and humanist values is a very flawed one. Liberal society is a society paralyzed by fear, intoxicated by its own decadence. Putin knows how weak we are, populists are waiting for their chance, our leaders keep us silent.

Art world suckers:
sucking on a merit by positions, rather than pushing the agenda of progressive culture

Art is an economy of luxury, of an extra both in being given the luxury to make earnings in art, or to be able to spend money on art. Meanwhile imagination and expression should be human rights, should be given to all naturally. Yet, aside from the economy of luxury, it is also a luxury to spend time in making art or being involved with art in whatever form. This framework creates not only the division between what people call amateur artists and professional artists, but also the division between people involved in art and those who are not.

Those not involved might knowingly miss the involvement or might not be aware or simply be too distant to feel this missing. This feeling of missing out on the artworld, is urgent to those who aspire to be a professional – that is a paid- career most. To these people, the evident need to be involved, is at friction with the opportunities to be involved. This is not simply a matter of not being paid but goes even deeper where it is a matter of personal insecurity, both in (not) having the material conditions but most of all in being unsure if one's personal involvement will have enough capacity. This is evidently most urgent from within a position with less access.

Meanwhile there is an art world out there. One with privileged positions living up to societal standards of the neoliberal regime, having the means to be fully involved by the position they have, and there are those freelance art workers, trying to sustain their basis and remain true to their work and to the cultural commitment that being involved in art brings along as immaterial result. This group holds a minimum of side jobs when necessary. This group invests much risk, both personally in who they are and what they can bring to engage within arts, as materially in the precarious nature of their living conditions.

Where amateurs, by consequence of not taking full risk, are less likely to be engaged, the semi-professionals are in constant struggle of feeling accepted in their personal risk brought along by their work and are in constant struggle to survive.

Psychologically speaking this pressure brings along a huge push to find a position. People need to balance their beliefs and outputs with the merit of the established art world. By nature, artistic practice is highly personal. This brings along a vocabulary which is very dear to the author. Consequently, it may be difficult not to be blinded by what you could call a personal, professional deformation. Equally and simultaneously, there is a gap between the freedom of the individual practitioner, working from high-density urgency to the frameworks of the established which are more conservative by nature, as established implies a basis of less risk and less unicity.

This does not imply the work of the non-established is unique, but implies their position is more singular. But, if the work is unique, it also holds a political position towards the established since it is deviant. Whether the work is poetical, political, symbolic or whatever, it is both singular and unique and differentiates. This is an act, a cultural act, and holds content. That is what makes it political. It is relevant that these vocabularies find a way, even where these singular people are hesitant to let go of their close and safe vocabularies.

Being committed and true to unicity and singularity is a huge effort these people bring. While living materially precarious, there is a huge push to find a position. Here people are tempted to become corrupted by authority and convention, mostly through the bearing of the merit of the established. People show up at openings elegantly dressed, talk with patrons who are in a completely disbalanced position and might even self-censor themselves.
At the same time there is a fear of missing out. Especially amongst students who both have tremendous energy and arrogance of youth, as well as amongst starting and mid-careers who feel they need to talk the right language. This brings up a huge culture on its own by generating an economy of discourse, often remote to the actual conduct of art. This is the economy of expert groups, of counseling, of advisors' etcetera.

Push for a position

FOMO

48

Aspiring to become an artist making a living out of art and remaining at a level where you can live out of art is probably the most difficult professional aspiration. The field of art at large, with its curators, writers and all related is a small field, vulnerable to political conjuncture.
And then, there is most money where art is a sphere of authority. This is happening in a small segment of culture, where people who have money seek cultural dandyism of sorts, rather than progressive attitudes. In the West rich baby-boomers make up a fair deal of this culture. Although unconsciously, they follow Bourdieu's notion of cultural capital which they take for granted with utmost decadence. In most cultures, it is really rich people showing off with exclusive stuff. In all cases, art is often ending up an investment. None of this has anything to do with progressive cultural work.

Yet, people involved in the making of ethics through aesthetics, also know how to dress. They look good, are fucking trendsetters, and thereby kind of the wished for best friend of the rich who are the powerful. Perhaps these trendsetters should just hire themselves as friends for these folks. But that is too sad in making this dependency as banal as it secretively already is.

Where the rich go to parties and places of art in their fancy cars, artists come by transport and walk a while, perhaps carrying something they could put on show of sorts. And then there is the polite way of conversating, the Americanization if you will: *'hi how are you?'*

Where there is an evident painfulness to the artist as the most precarious worker, this painfulness is even more striking for curators. They need to build networks as freelancers, suck up in diplomatic words. Say 'they are so proud to be dadadadada', or 'so honored to be dadadadada'. It stinks. Often, they show themselves with photos of them wearing fancy clothes, even a suit, and at times even sitting on a designers' sofa or something: dressed in aesthetics that shows no ethics but dandyism and elitism. But once institutionalized, people build up pensionships and more... They will never be equals on the table with artists again. They will hardly have the liberty to engage in progressive cultural production.

Progressive cultural work can only be produced independently, that is supported by a state elected by voters who want to live free and progressive. This is the same for academia at large, from the arts to chemistry, medicine etc etc and perhaps most of all: economics.

Loon naar werken – welk werk?

Pay to work – what work?

Work is not to self-preserve, but to be in the world. Fair pay cannot restrict itself to working sectors or geopolitical boundaries.

Yet, this is what we're faced with.

But progressive cultural workers don't care. They work because they are committed to the work, to produce culture progressively.

They save and reinvest where possible, they do not count hours at all because it is not about hours but living your life okay. Hours can never be paid according to any fucking standard anyway. So leave that bullshit to the greedy.

(we are all social democrats under capitalism now)

Aside from the self-marinization by rhetoric of punk and entrepreneurship there is the self-marginalization by social democratic laws in the neoliberal regime.

People with good intentions feel left out within the neoliberal regime. Civil respectful work being under or unpaid should be paid fair, artistic work appreciated being under or unpaid should be paid fair, working cultures should respect social values, need to listen to and learn from everyone.

Often people say a worker should keep up dignity by saying no. But independent work, which will always be precarious, will therefore become more costly and more time consuming if the only people saying yes are those gaining full budgets. This means there will be less work paid better and working cultures remaining in better circumstances. Furthermore: often people say a worker should keep up dignity by saying no, even when a worker feels the work needs to be released. This means people who feel like they need to do something should accept not being able to release their voice, even when they feel it is needed. In consequence we can legitimately ask ourselves who will turn out to claim the independent voice? I dare to argue it will be office holders; people in a privileged position.

The office holders respond to needs for more horizontal floors and inclusive cultures by harnessing bureaucracy in work meetings, think thanks, feedback sessions and evaluations all along endless scripts which are endless topics of negotiation to start out with. This all takes away energy from actual work, which should be the emancipating of the silent majority by reaching out to them independently. The objective is to make a culture of being independent, being resistant without losing capacity to get things done. Now it almost seems as if getting things going equals getting things done. It's not: it is a social democratic tissue from a neoliberal hat supporting capitalism.

And you know what: this again and exactly is where the neoliberal is applying the hidden practice of social democracy to silence the independent; to chain them. This is extra visible when we look at the geopolitics of nations, for is Bulgaria even able to support this level, or is Hungary even willing for just a little bit? No: it is the decadence of the most western states, where wellbeing is synonymous with rights claimed by the people's sovereign as the people's sovereign is neoliberal in minimum, right wing extreme in max. Putin knows, and that is how he tries to divide and conquer. So why does the silent majority's leaders in these people sovereignties allow for more codes: to make them office holders, chaining them to their mortgages and more while they are being drawn in under the veil of the rhetoric of a supposedly independent grassroot movement.

Meanwhile the legitimate need is for a clarity beyond the rhetoric of political opportunism to the people's sovereignty and beyond the silence practiced by the merit of collective consciousness. As the merit of neoliberal capitalism brings enough social democracy to tie the independent on the leash of eternal bureaucracy, leaving the independent worker nothing but 'expert-based' meetings as work, the silence is protected. We should not speak with each other but should reach out to others. The market for the marginal and independent is not with their friends, but with their enemies. If not, they stick to their our own little 'audiences', feasting on this as 'work'.

care part

Care in the neoliberal regime was a secretive call to self-interests. In the national conservative days, it claims so explicitly.

Care rests upon

- standing in solidarity, not with your fellow man or workers, but with those excluded by your own power.
- not about the here and now, but about sustainability from past to present and future.
- not about geopolitical but about practicing solidarity
- not about protectionism but about giving
- not about self-care but caring for the collective mission
- organizing the independent
- more of such

Care is about the other, not about oneself. Even progressive cultural workers in the West are privileged, and they know. It is the people who ignore their privilege who fail.

Care means you don't care about yourself along the standards of decadence.

Therefore, practicing care should NOT look at what progressives can do to better themselves or bring nuance to their work, but should be about creating dialogues with those in power, without sucking up and getting corrupt.

There should not be expert meetings of progressive workers dwelling in self-pity, shame and inability;they should take action. They should not share symbolic acts amongst each other but try and push those who fail to care.

‘Public responsibility’

Public responsibility is not just the pointing of a finger. What we address when we speak of 'public responsibility' is really the need to regulate and deregulate, for that is what a public structure brings.
Communism promotes controlling government, social democracy promotes socially wide government, neoliberalism promotes a wide but technocratic government, liberal politics (which is different from the liberal in liberal democracy) promotes small government.

Independent culture requires, in my view, a liberal democracy wherein the state grants the access of the marginal and rejects both silence and majorities. The liberal in democracy as well as independence, rests on the freedoms of its inhabitants. If these inhabitants are liberal in themselves, they will not fall prey to any decadence and protectionism from the small and exclusive of liberal politics up to the egalitarian repression of communism.

In the technocratic regime of neoliberal capitalism such as in the Netherlands, we see governments promoting themselves along their own agenda's, mostly economically motivated. They promote to different audiences with sometimes contradictory voices. Policy is likewise made up along the stakes of many. This enforces the big state of the neoliberal, and ties it together with elements of social democracy. Likewise in cultural policy. This big state adapts to political cycles and becomes more complex along these cycles, extra more within the layered support of stakeholders where ideological lines are blurring continuously as focus points shifts. In cultural policy these shifts range from more to less centralization, more to less social democratic conditions and bureaucracy but overall, the leash of public support in cultural policy is enforced by dependence to financial means and responsibility to regulations by conditions set. The more these conditions prescribe the work, the politics to this prescribing is part in the accepting of the work. This may corrupt to self-censor, either more or less, to the work's result.

It is a formal fact that public responsibility rests with public services, led by politicians led by people in democracies. It is not the politicians who are to blame, but the peoples' voting. Yet it is the politicians, particularly in a parliamentary system, who have much executive responsibility. That is why people vote strategically or give up voting. Meanwhile, where the politician's policy's strength is reliant on many forces, the dissemination of policy to public services takes time, and will also have its own construct. Deep cultural change, particularly in cultures of public services where silence is the key in a merit of stability for workers and working cultures, takes time.

Cultural production in the neoliberal order are inherently geopolitical interest. The nation stimulated national artists and designers, also in expanding abroad to stimulate export / financial results floating into the country and cultural interest / cultural imperialism. Dutch Design for instance could be considered a conceptual shift in design but could equally be considered a state supported program to put a Dutch identity on the map. Architecture has benefited greatly even if working in dictatorial China for instance. Same with regional interests to try and deal with provincialism by stimulating wellbeing or trying to deal with pride for better or worse. Cities promoting themselves, needing culture to brand and bread and play for the people. Europe was an interesting version of this, as European funding brough people and cultures together, not to elevate segregation like the interests of nations, regions and cities, but to meet and exchange. It helped progressive cultural dynamics in Eastern Europe to sustain, it connected neighbors in Europe to build relationships, imagine their politics and landscapes etcetera.

Up to the big 2012 budget cuts, Dutch policy spoke of 'spreiding', meaning they intended to have culture available throughout the country, including provincial places usually named 'the province'. This naming already expresses how much they were lacking actual engagement. Most committee members were based in the cutural centre of the Netherlands called 'De Randstad'. This had various faces, including a good one that pushed for a level of quality, but also bad ones in that they did not understand sensitivities in making, in showing, in the way to engage peripheral audiences. At present provincialism took ruling over the bar. There once was the opportunity to engage people in setting levels of bars, now it is just leveling (meaning a levelling down). This also complicates connectivity between funding bodies supporting national, regional and local interest. But it does not mean the idea of spreiding is bad. In fact: it was a really good ambition as funding is to support the basis of our democracy: the voters.

But yeah... with the rise of national conservatism, cultural policy will become bread and play, it will be stimulating the interest of conservative pride and glory.

Bricks and mortar

Producing cultural production as public service is vulnerable to the costs of space. Much public funding goes out to 'stones' as the Eindhoven alderwoman of culture once tried to address. But then they came up with placemaking, including all that bullshit rhetoric wherein creatives renovate, move, install, and start all over again. I always refused this.

Once I sat with a new alderwoman of culture, who asked what I brought to the city. I mentioned the organization I directed did not get local funding, but got funding from all other governments and more, paid an annual 60.000 euro on rent and have no permanent contracts as we only As we only received programme based funding. She felt silent, not knowing. But never heard from her again.
Same for big institutions like museums, who build to become postcard material locals are supposed to be proud of, including big entry halls with crazy costs of heating.

To progressive cultural producers, this situation means they have to save somehow to build capital to purchase real estate. Renting is no option, as you will be moved around all the time. Just look at the stability of W139 in Amsterdam, who owns the building, opposite to De Appel, who moved around as they were vulnerable in their locations' costs.

Somehow the costs of space have to be resistant both to political / funding conjuncture and find basis in independent earnings. That is really difficult, perhaps the biggest challenge to institutions on the lower end of the regime, but a necessity to keep the work–and therefore positions for workers–secure.

Yet, maintenance is required. Who doesn't know of collective buildings, studio buildings falling apart. It is only by proper management, and proper independent ownership, that this can sustain itself. Once initiated by artist Bridget Riley and Peter Sledge, the London/Uk organization Space is an example of self-ownership. Sadely, marginal's seldomly have the required funding, particularly in areas where real estate is booming

Cultural discourse as a rightful product of capitalist logic, now under threat.

Expert meetings, conferences, coaching sessions: where consultancy as externally hired expertise in government took over authority and hardly brought anything apart from a moment of false creative empowerment to people who are there to get their hands dirty. There are many freelancers and institutional professionals in culture joining up in places to gather and talk, often with the same people on similar topics. This has become an industry, reproducing and producing authority and legitimized by the idea of the knowledge economy. To involve freelancers, some of which become hyped stars, helps building a practice. For institutional workers it helps create an aura of tolerance and self-research, sometimes support. This is increased by the growth of the PhD industry. In a way this is leftish academia, formerly there to bring support to the social democratic component in neoliberalism. Making stars or bringing authority to these people was relevant, as it brought relative safety to these ideas in a neoliberal regime. But presently, under conservative nationalism, it is not safe anymore.

The only way for this discourse to reach beyond the confines of leftish scenes and academia, is to be branded better and brought to the masses. To come out of its bunkers and take all risk trying to move beyond the precarious cultures formerly known as institutional safe havens. This should have happened a long time ago, and there is still a long way to go in improving the populist ways of criticality, but there must be a moment to get this started. People producing must see what they can do. And be aware: the current situation for discourse might be more exclusive to the most committed voices, and radicalization might follow from this. That would be a pity as we have to see how to mediate our voices and gestures.

The aesthetics of criticism

Criticism fails itself when it dresses up as a crappy form of Vivianne Westwood. Or not even stronger: when it looks like it got pulled out of the drunken-ass of someone shouting he's an anarchist while he sucks up to his equally wasted dog, being his only true friend.
Same for communications. if you become too intellectual, not even intellectuals will know what you're talking about.
Same for artistic autonomy: if there are no conditions to a gesture, it loses any grounds to have any saying.
In all these cases, progressive cultural production fails.

Now: I'm not saying there is a clear-cut answer, just saying this should be avoided. There's also no space for pride: pride is something for Putin riding a horse bare-chested or so, but not for progressive cultural workers. Pride is a remnant of a paternalistic era.
Things can never be about pride, but only about critical connection. Pride is protectionist, pride is closed.
Pride is for losers.

Therefore, aesthetics should not be fixed. Identities cannot be fixated. The identities of boring but well-placed type design are simply expressing the authority of a dead culture. Equally designers working with single typefaces only, are afraid to be vulnerable.

Print is punk???

Fuck off please

Where the market decides over access to the market and neoliberal politics decides what is to be regulated or not, much work is not shared, much culture is not offered, much freedom is not made available.
It is here that a DIY economy fuelled by precarious work is needed.

But this economy should not be self-oriented or corrupt. It should believe in the value of the culture they bring. But this is often not the case. Within the independent publishing scenes there's a strong culture of self-marginalisation.
This shows itself negatively wrapped as 'attitude' to sustain the energy while spitting to all others. Here, print as punk becomes a gimmick of itself, eroding its inner qualities to something outcasted or even easily to be commercially hijacked as a pastiche of itself. Saying 'fuck you' does not say shit, and neither opens much. Evidently design has fully become a tool to the 'generosity' of 'the product', and the design realm has been claimed by capitalism. But this is where people feel safe: in the reproduced identity of global similar coffee-bar hospitality. But the content is never to be claimed. So please be a wolf in sheep clothes.
On another line, independent culture shows itself corrupt where it positions (not promotes) itself as niche for selected audiences, thus accepting the neoliberal regimes' rhetoric and agenda of entrepreneurship repressing the marginal. Independence is relevant

to all. When introductory lines and titles are weakened by the corruption of neoliberal rhetoric, they do not claim independence and quality they hold, and subsequently do not respect the people (people not audience for we should not turn free souls into clients, or even worse 'audiences', for we should not discriminate). The difficult (rather than vague as difficult is positive and vague disqualifies along capitalist merit and excludes curiosity) and conflicting (rather than opposing which renounces) are to be embraced for their potentiality and the effort brought. It is not consumption, which is desired, but criticality. It is not affirmation, which is desired, but negotiation.
In a world where the collective consciousness of the majority is left silent, the silence of the majority is left incapable of dealing with negotiation. As the silent majority thus builds people's sovereignty's build on narrow minds, which easily force marginals to fundamentalism. To reason with them, and be respectful to this majority, means we need to reconsider their terms. Meanwhile the independent must find a place alongside of the merit of the silent majority, subverting it and changing culture at large.

Depatriarchising the book

I value criticality towards authority and convention, not the least as this mostly is not relevant to readers and should not be relevant to readers. Authority slips in through formalized traditions and habits, often coming out of a fear for missing out, either personal or institutional.

Institutions particularly fall into these traps, as it is professional to list and represent institutions in certain ways. Clear examples are a wish or even demand to be mentioned as publisher, while they do not get the formal listing as the ISBN is registered with the actual publisher and the distribution runs through the publisher. With publishing, there can be only one, unless another publisher serves the distribution in another region, and you apply another ISBN and barcode for that. But institutions still wish to be mentioned as publishers. Like phantom limbs of authority and claiming to be something they are not. So basically, it is just false noise if you find this on a book cover. Another example can be found when entering the book. Often the first thing you run into is a word from the director, thanking patrons and bla bla bla. Nobody gives a shit. It is not about that. Just write an honest thanks in the back of the book. Only people who don't know who they are, want to be represented as people in a prominent, misplaced position. List the colophon with care, mention actual work and consider the naming of that work: try and be true, perhaps

in a creative way. Don't drop functions because they sound well. Same with logos. They are ugly, disrupt the flow and claim a superficial mark at a place where it corrupts the actual work they want to support. Speak by actions, not by claims, I'd say. Just put them in the colophon, where people look at authority bullshit, or to find the names of people entitled to get actual credits.
If you want to credit people in the book or be take responsibility over how it was conceived either managing and/or in content transfer, write a responsibility, an honest word of thanks or something like that.

But so far for the obvious authority.

There is another authority which is perhaps more hidden. The traditional structure of the book, stemming from classic literature and academia, has a narrative from beginning to end, from introduction to conclusion. Often edited content of assembled contributors ends up in a container of that content, from A to Z, without further consideration of what that content brings. You can see this in the way the table of contents is presented, and in how the book is laid out. Editorials and post-produced (after content assembling) meta-narratives can speak up for the actual overall contents of the book provide many opportunities. People don't read books from A to Z. You can make it more diagonal, provide various entries, work with the book format in considering the dissemination of these narratives. The book is an interface of the content it provides.

For artists–I mean visual artists here–a book often is supposedly better if the images are larger, if the image quality is best in mirroring the work and so on. Sometimes artists even believe glossier is better. Desires for textual embedding are often limited, as the work speaks by itself. It is too easy, but all curators are able to make a book filled with many artworks that look like scribbles, or a book filled with works that look like monochromes (perhaps in a color gradient) and so on. Work only resonates if someone would be interested in that particular scribble of monochrome and is already aware of the work. Otherwise, it is just plain arrogance that supports the inaccessibility and bullshit-ness of art. It is therefore disrespectful to the artist to make such a book, unless you want to be marginalized. But why should such book be made with public funding... In these cases, they make coffee table books for galleries, targeting rich and dependent people. Let them pay for something exclusive.

You could say stepping out of these zones is depatriarching. I think so and experience it that way. I also think the creative work that follows from this, very much opens to tolerance and new registers. This is where creativity should be: at the edges of our comfort zones, looking at what we can do better with the means available. You could say this is queering, as it explores alternative ways of breathing space for and with the book. But this label is too fancy I'd say, as there are also conventions within queer cultures. In the end it is about practicing freedom I'd say, a classic liberal act, where you must work through the opportunities of all resources available: manpower, spirits and matter. Being both critical, tolerant and effective is vital to get stuff going. In the end the world is still run by vampires drinking our blood, so little pragmatism doesn't do any harm to create more basis.

Opportunities brought to the table may be good, but if they become a pain or a burden, just don't drop them and either let go of the project a little or completely, unless you are paid well and really need the money. It isn't easy.

Every book will have its own opportunities and shortcomings, demanding more or demanding less, but all options demanded might not always end up on the table. People won't know unless they look at the result from a bookmakers' point of view. And that point of view is irrelevant as only the work speaks to the audience.

ps.
the same dynamics more or less apply to curating.

Fashion victims and/or social fabrics
People's validation

(text as published in 2011)

"When a woman alters her look too much from season to season, she becomes a fashion victim."
- Gianni Versace (fashion designer)

"To put it more provocatively, I would argue that design is one of the terms that has replaced the word "revolution"! To say that everything has to be designed and redesigned (including nature), we imply something of the sort: "it will neither be revolutionised, nor will it be modernised." For me, the word design is a little tracer whose expansion could prove the depth to which we have stopped believing that we have been modern. In other words, the more we think of ourselves as designers, the less we think of ourselves as modernisers."
- Bruno Latour (anthropologist and sociologist)

"Today, more people are interested in image production then image contemplation."
- Boris Groys (philosopher)

At the end of history – at least 20th-century history – both human culture as non human nature seem to have mobilised fully to equip an industry by and for the fashionable. We bluntly conceive its economy effectively as suppliers, producers, advertisers, facilitators or consumers. These various roles level up different forms of authorisation that qualify or quantify the values involved in this economy. To some, these forms might be out of sight, to others they might be within the scope of their horizon and to some it might be the same (old) stuff. As individuals, we could feel left out as we experience some kind of lack. Or we could feel resistant as we feel the necessity to inform or activate others. Mostly we just don't care, as "there's too much we could care about and we already have so much on our minds"... Overall to this economy, "common sense" is more intrusive as reason[*].

The above scenarios draft various personal stances as bases for economic validation on the grounds of a subjective point of view and experience. It's not so much a coward's "eye of the beholder" argument as it is an indicator of the economic extent to which we're able to conceive and manage this economy of our authentic experiences. We truly are left on our own when it comes to the way we do or don't relate. This doesn't mean we should turn towards fatalism or even cynicism; we should enter the economic arena with dignity and self-respect. Effectively it means we'd have to play in between the power and reasoning of both high- and low-culture.

Within this very fracture of high and low, two currents design a rather flexible and open body of signification. First of all: the authority and reign of high-culture fades. Recently the Netherlands experienced an upheaval of the construct of a national canon; a high-cultural, top-down paradigm that would artificially construct a framework for people's understanding of their shared identity. It's not surprising these ideas specifically manifest themselves in the fields of history and literature, also touching upon philosophy and, effectively, politics. Simultaneously, there have been debates on the construction of a European constitution that "should" be based upon enlightened thought, Jewish-Christian heritage and such. Literature and history are logical players in the call for a meaningful identity, for they are able to trace and pinpoint cultural values, despite the simple fact that hardly anyone would be able to read all the books or understand all ideas proposed.

We don't construct our lives; we practice them. High-cultural wise-guys should acknowledge that rationality does not run life. Effectively, mass media and pop culture are the real axis, assisting us in practising identity.

Secondly: the alteration in labour relations caused by technological advancement and globalisation. We work anywhere and anytime, we utilise virtual tools and deal with real person on the other end of the connection, physically, potentially, anywhere. In this very arena we need to compete effectively, for national borders can't supply a safe haven.
Therefore, our body of being is rather subject-based:

partially specifically equipped, partially naïve. We can't blame ourselves. Still it's within this sphere that we have to act and have to take on the responsibility to make decisions. "A populist judgement on art such as 'Anyone could do this' expresses the discrepancy between the visual appearance of modern art and its institutional status." (Seijdel, 2010, p. 43). Still, that doesn't imply that we should start and bash intellectuals. Smart guys might in fact have smart stuff to say. But not only that: "Anyone could do this" would be argued by someone who would, "like anyone", follow the fashion of the day: it's within this very culture that both high- and low-culture generate their fashionable lure and victims of war.

"Both in professional traffic as in case of the consuming audience specific qualities are vital, like flexibility, mobility, communication, virtuosity, informality, performativity and potentiality." (Seijdel, 2010, p. 62) In the end we all live up to the same range of temptations showcased. What about the successes of the "high" culture namedropping of philosopher Jacques Rancière?: he speaks like shit, his writings are not really accessible though he has nice ideas on sensibilities. What about the success of the "low" culture namedropping of Lady Gaga?: she's a copy of David Bowie and Madonna. The reason for their effect must be that we crave the idea of an original author who actually offers a sphere beyond, within the present.

Effectively: the feeling of being part of something larger than life.

Eventually, everyone can be a professional as well as an amateur: some people do appreciate both Ranci-ère as well as Gaga. What we want to experience are "true emotions", so it sells.

It's in this field, that commercial values and cultu-ral values become one and the same. This not only economically "happening": we also live this, as it becomes the social fabric of life. Suddenly, we can all act highly cultural and lowly cultural and use the communicative and rhetorical sensibilities for better or for worse. 'Don't be cool. Cool is conservative fear dressed in black. Free yourself from limits of this sort.' (Bruce Mau, axiom #14 in An incomplete manifesto for growth)

Cultural practice became a practice of commerce; of a turnover of the identity of the person or the subject. While previously we wanted to activate the market through efforts to generate "responsible producers" or "active consumers", we now have to activate huma-nist citizenship, for every human can take every role. There have been some predecessors to this, in the form of "outsiders" commenting on scientific research or artists taking the perspective and position of the amateur. Mostly, cross-disciplinary practices seem to be a rather viable profession. This is only logical, for if we would not be able to make at least some translation between various positions, we'd completely lose track of each other. As such, all human beings are not committed to any social contract but are living within a moral contract. We can disagree but have to follow the rules of lawfulness and democracy. Indeed: people do sometimes argue, but 'it is a mistake not to recognise conflictual collaboration as the primary means through which ideas and innovation are generated. The challenge is to build relations and points of connection that enable a plurality of research platforms and small business alternatives that can survive beyond the initial consensus model of the three month incubators.' (Lovink & Rossiter, 2007, p.10)

As such, I'd like to argue that this morally agreed dissent acts exactly upon this cultural-commercial axis. It can build upon this as it allows people to respect and acknowledge their experiences as well as their reason. It's a play of signification: not of an image economy of material stuff outside of our experiences, that showcases or elaborates the politics of the visual; nor is it a complete and configured sum of expressed and balanced communication brought to us through authorship. It's a play beyond aesthetics and poetics, beyond high and low. Effectively, it's a subject's play of motivation and expression. Life does not come about via hermeneutics, neither is it a simple saturation of pop. We only require more awareness of the need for conflict and the trust required.

Literature:

Groys, B. (2010). Going Public. Berlin: Sternberg Press.

Lovink, G. & Rossiter, N. (red.) (2007). MyCreativity Reader. Amsterdam: Institute of Network Cultures.

Seijdel, J. (2010). De waarde van de amateur. Amsterdam: Fonds BKVB.

Tilder, L. & Blostein, B. (red.) (2010). Design Ecologies. New-York: Princeton Architectural Press.

Stakes and responsibilities of rhetoric's within contemporary culture's design realm

(text as published in 2018)

I don't read books by people who have betrayed the Motherland. In the modern world, those who are weak will get unambiguous advice from foreign visitors which way to go and what policy course to pursue. In many countries today, moral and ethical norms are being reconsidered; national traditions, differences in nation and culture are being erased. We must stop using the language of force and return to the path of civilized diplomatic and political settlement. Europeans are really dying out!'
'The taste of 34% curvy carrot, 40% awesome apple, 12% beautiful banana, 2% loving lemon, 12% optimistic orange': 100% best drink ever. The sublime-sepia landscape-window comforts custom-style as the 80%-electronic car slides through. The car says I should not get too excited, as my increased heartbeat got noticed. Am I dreaming my dream . . . 'if not now, then when'. So 'let's celebrate the new'. 'Persistence is fruitful if you follow your gut'. 'There is much beauty in loss'. 'Trust strangers'. 'Make your own reality'. 'Harness nature's hidden superpowers'. 'Nature is everywhere; we just need to learn to see it'. 'The next manufacturing revolution is here'. 'We can learn from shortcuts'. 'Better tech protects us from distraction'. 'Math is sexy'. 'Barbershops keep man healthy'. 'We can reprogram life'. 'Less is more'. As I close the screen of my laptop, I fall asleep.[1]

The above story does not acknowledge the daily

[1] Italic part consists in quotes from Wladimir Putin, juice packaging, Titles of TED-lectures, Dutch Design Week promo-slogans and some little sentences to fill up the story.

routine that determines our life: the need to work – in order to shop – in order to serve ourselves food – in order to sleep well – in order to work well. Moving beyond the day-to-day matters of fact filling our routine, the above text is full of claims and suggestions to truths beyond that make our days promising.[2] It is the promise beyond matters of fact that offer opportunities both to contribute to a better world and to live a better world. This is why the suggested truth beyond is more promising than the matters of fact.

In this essay I want to discuss the way truths are sourced and how this sourcing reflects the foundation of our contemporaneity, consider its vitality and, accordingly, consider how to approach this.

First of all, I will do so by proposing two forms of truth, the 'innovative truth' and the 'open truth' as a think model to think through and re-experience the motivation wherein we are inclined to portray and engage our reality. As such, it anticipates to the gut of our lower belly, in an attempt to inform and inspire.

'Innovative truth'

Some sources of suggested truth are good at producing a truth of social construction, of societal feasibility. This is the domain of structural planners and producers: sociologists, architects, politicians and industrial designers. They make 'our world' (the horizontal world of all people) vertically better. These paternalists guide our path, by professional capacity

[2] At least if we are one of the lucky few celebrating a 'good life'.

and by sincere commitment.

This truth I would like to label ‘innovative truth’, as it is a prophesy of improvement, sparked by professional development. It only exists within the public domain, as ready-to-feed rhetorical prophesy of populism immersing concerned target groups. As such it might be segregated in its approach to various audiences, yet is horizontal, as all masses, at any societal layer, might have been succumbed. It leaves promoted ‘innovation’ a static conception of truth; passive to those entangled in its web. The innovative truth is a paternalistic truth appropriated to fit the elite’s agenda, be it for better or worse. My problem is not so much the positive or negative result it might produce but rather its fundamental working.

‘Open truth’

On the other end there is the ‘open truth’. This is a truth at best: an experimental truth and therefore a truth of a dynamic order. This truth is, surely in the public arena, to be approved rather than proven. It is vertical in itself, as it is to be contested at all times, yet it is available to all and in that fundamentally horizontal.

The face of truth encountered here has not been produced but is to be produced; it is process based, sparked by the quest to find and experiment rather than fixate and impose. Living this truth, we become artists and philosophers. It is a moral truth that roots in opportunities for emancipated citizenship and living, be it for better or worse.

Changes

Around the turn of the millennium, our conception of truth started to change. By connecting databases, the complexity of the growing knowledge economy grew further and further from the average person, alienating everyone from self-governance in society compartmentalised by virtually connected networks. No one, not even politicians supposed be generic control freaks, could follow up. In our wish to contribute to feasibility for a better, we stared Googling and checking up YouTube tutorials. The amateur-professional became a societal actor. Independent vlogging took over the signalling role of independent research journalism, medical advice was to be found online, political debate moved to the domain of 'reaguurders' (ed. Dutch word for Internet forum bashers). It wasn't that information democratised, but rather the network for producing and using information – the 'library', so to say – that democratised. In this, the authority of academia fell. A rise of anti-intellectualism resulted. Yet – and this is fascinating – access to information fell in its 'public' cause (public as in 'public library').

Sources

The new 'public library' was taken over by two major power blocks, which unfortunately did not deliver a site for and of an 'open truth'. . . On the one end there came global capitalism with Google, Baidu, Facebook and all alike, segregating along the currents of its content, preaching to the likes. This eradicated conflict and diversity and an economic exploitation along a global levelling of identity. All coffee bars worldwide are covered by wood sanded in some half-done manner, labelled by a kind of early industrial typeface and such. The standardised prophesy of wellbeing is the supposed truth sold as capitalisms' wet dream, leaving indoctrination to the users. This global economic imperialism imposes capitalist culture worldwide.[3] On the other end, in opposition to capitalism, we see the rise of strong leadership promoting the geopolitical by naturalistic right. Proposed by incapable politicians, unable to overcome the globalisation of networks within their little geopolitical nation-states, they promote their story equally narrow-mindedly. Both the retro rhetoric of geopolitical-local roots and the futurist rhetoric of Gleichschaltung for capitalist well-being scales up the prophesy of 'innovative truth'. We all feel threatened by these supposedly independent forces. This threat to truth is even reaching a level wherein conspiracy theories of the most insane kind are becoming accepted.

[3] Now, this is typical Dutch: we are highly developed technocrats by centuries of colonialism and post-colonialism. We are silenced by 'gezelligheid' (unique untranslatable Dutch word for something like indifferent social cosiness) and we are obsessed by 'making things better' (former Philips slogan fitting Dutch culture that has no problems because we are problem-solvers . . .).

Vitality

Uncertainty is not convincing, I know. Yet we need to build in more uncertainty within our culture and the economy that produces it. We need places where we can talk about doubts, expand upon doubts, produce doubt better and so on. We need to live an open truth as true innovation lies outside of the box. Politics and commerce are highly unlikely to invest in this. Patents, copyrights and the like hold back on open access (increasing the distrust to power and intelligentsia). It is vital to find access to information in the independent. Art to produce cultural experience and academia producing cultural thought. It is here that the independent becomes a vehicle in parallel to politics and capitalism: a platform able to distribute opportunity to explore the contemporary, both in hindsight and towards the days and future to come, as well in local as global perspective.

For this reason, we have to distrust the creative industries, as it is there, that 'creativity' becomes a rhetorical vehicle producing promoting a participatory rhetoric of bread and play – as is most evident in the style of capitalist social housing companies gentrifying neighbourhoods. This is applied almost by naturalist law, as the strong and powerful survive4. On the other hand, 'creativity' lies in the capitalist sales of feminism conditioned by Beyoncé, of design-craft conditioned by Pharrell Williams or of anarchy conditioned by H&M.

By the sheer force and mass of their productive capacity and public outreach, the independent and thus an open truth is not allowed access to the market they promote. And more, the legal system does not compensate as politicians and their administration make the law to the system they produced: this is the reason why neoliberalism failed its regulative prophesy.

On 10/31/2016 19:41 Studio XXX <studio@XXX.com> wrote:
Hello Freek,
Thank you so much for coming back to me:)
I'm writing you from the art fair in Cologne where project XXXX are exhibited among 10 the finalists of XXXX Art Award.
You can see how it looks on my Instagram: XXXX
If you don't mind I have few questions and your answers would help me a lot:
1. What would be your advice for a young artist to start with? What is the way of showing your work and getting noticed by curators?
2. I believe that one of the best ways to get visible is taking part in Art Competitions, Awards, etc. Could you name a few that are worth checking?
All the best,

XXXX
On 10/31/2016 21:31 PM, Freek Lomme/(in) dependent curator and writer wrote:
i don't care about awards to be honest. I simply want to consider the quality of work. You did not ask me a question in your first email and did not describe the work but only stated that it was widely covered and such non-information. Just say what you do, what you want your work to do, show it in the documentation, possibly supported by experiences of users/audience/professionals. References without motivation are bullshit as well. People who follow authority are stupid. If you want people to suck up, you make the world a worse place. Personally i do not like arrogant people as well, because that complicates an open conversation. I prefer specific questions that challenge me within the field i cover and feel it is most relevant to contact me with such questions. Your question is very generic, so the fact that i answer shows my respect for a question asked.
So my suggestion to young practitioners in the end is to make relevant work, do it well and propose to specific people with clear questions.
it is a pity that capitalism turns creative people into showoffs of finished accomplishments. Creativity is open, is tolerant, is dualis-

tic, is dynamic, is never finished. . .
greetings
Freek

Approach

Again, we are living a bipolar international arena wherein two regimes are in friction to one another, each on its own held together by indoctrination. If the consumer within capitalist society does not capitulate first, then the citizen within a political society will. Under the semblance of being locally anchored and globally positioned, excluded from an open truth, people should take charge over systems again. This ignites by informing ourselves on the literacy of its rhetoric, expands by distributing the information on rhetoric more widely and, finally, by reconstructing the order by takeover of its rhetoric. There are still opportunities for humanist dissent and independent production. The enlightenment produced by emancipation very much rests on fundamental knowledge produced in a vibrant sphere in Kaliningrad: a city whose citizens are currently troubled by EU borders in their drive to neighbouring city Gdansk. These citizens could possibly become Estonian e-citizens though . . .
There is no responsibility to the rhetoric of a system. Responsibility is reserved to an open structure, an agora; built upon an inclusive diversity of people.

Balancing ethics and economies: A push for a new perspective on art publishing

(text as published in 2021)

The culture of independent publishing and forms of self-publishing has grown in recent times, into an industry that makes a serious contribution to the global publishing economy; in turn these developments have changed the landscape of broader art publishing.
In this text, I will describe changes to this publishing infrastructure and raise some of the most urgent challenges in order to foster this economy and consider how publishers can balance ethics and integrity with the competing demands on book production. I hope this honest text enables independent writers, publishers, or designers interested in bookmaking to see their ambitions more clearly, and for those currently engaged with the field to consider their responsibilities in responding to challenge. The economy I wish to refer to is, what I would call, progressive cultural publishing.

I write this text as Founding Director of Onomatopee, a publisher and a public gallery producing projects consisting of both public programs (exhibitions, lectures, workshops), which are services, and publishing, which produces products (books). I am only writing this as a testimony of my vision and agenda, on the basis of the experiences I had over the past 15 years. Through the Onomatopee projects we mediate between radicality, experimentation, the avant-garde, or alternative knowledge production. We aim to meet and be generous to an audience that is curious for something different and, as our founding principles suggest, to inspire cultural life more broadly. We fund these projects independently, through our exhibition program, commissions by institutions, cultural practitioners and academics and, evidently, publication sales.

As founding director of this small business–albeit not for profit–my experience is similar to that of a family business, who are often the backbone of economies. I know every aspect of the business by having done it thoroughly. I literally know how stuff works, where stuff is and how to keep stuff going or to keep making stuff go better. The chain of production is clear to me in all its components. Let me conclude this introduction with two relevant distinctions that help you understand the bottom line of this text.

Firstly, when I started Onomatopee with my friend, graphic designer Remco van Bladel, we were self-publishing. As we grew into the business and came to know of the various sources and capacities to include we became publishers. Where self-publishing is naïve, the practice of publishing is one where you know things, have more infrastructure, and can accordingly take on more responsibility.

Secondly, although I speak of books here, it could equally be any other alternative good or service of progressive nature with the capacity to circulate worldwide, and you can therefore equally think ‘books’ with ‘any alternative product or service’ in this text including knowledge and art writing.

The rise of the undercurrent within a global publishing economy

Traditionally art publishing mostly consists of monographic catalogues, with coffee-table print-specs, an introduction by a stakeholder claiming superiority of himself and the institution, an essay by an acclaimed critic or curator that reaffirms the quality of the product and so on. This book is usually produced by an elite who publish to support their own cultural accomplishments. Often, these books are not distributed in any commercial, or supply-chain sense that is common to the larger book trade and yet they are printed in relatively high numbers, to sell in their gift shops and give to their patrons. If they are distributed, they are often run through publishers such as Hatje Cantz or Lars Muller or gallerists such as Hauser & Wirth. This historical backbone of art publishing shapes the dominant perception of such publishing and is the everlasting economic backdrop of current progressive cultural publishing. For independent publishing to push to exist it has to both accept and reject the dominant sphere of art publishing to understand the conservative notion of the book and instead produce titles that align with the notion of an alternative book.

Around 2005, a group of independent publishers, academics, graphic designers and art workers such as myself started to form a culture and economy of independent publishing which slowly gained prominence on the margins of general art publishing's big business. At the time a commonality in this art press ecology was that one person performed many roles – from editing the publication, speaking to authors, designing the book, to selling drinks at the launch event. This ecology required each imprint to have a largely DIY approach to keep costs low, remain agile and have a high level of energy to produce these projects while still travelling, being part of events and remain able to distribute.

This ecology grew mid 2000's as small publishers took cheap flights to small art book fairs and events, found one another's blogs and paired up with distributors covering specific continents and interest areas. These distributors were based in Europe, North America, and Australia. Continents with the means and the infrastructure to take on small independent imprints producing specific art writing and discourse. It was through this internationalisation, using the waves of international global cultural capitalism, that independent culture could find more reach. Specific styles of books, types of writing and reader engagement meant these small publishers were able to increase print runs, and find more of a market themselves and obtain acquisitions for new titles, commissions and collaborations. This market, to most of these independents, meant more engagement rather than more money and for the most part relied on publishers giving a lot of time and effort to break into said market.

How It's Made'

A memory that strikes me, is one familiar in this ecology, the act of having to pack and carry books around the world to these art book events. This memory provides a tangible example of the perils of distribution:
'After consulting the internet, visiting stores to feel fabrics and check on wheels, one evening I started to order a North Face trolley on my mobile phone. Supposedly with the best wheels: 'in-line skating best-quality'. I need a trolley to carry books around with me. The need for a good one came out of too many bad trips caused by supposedly robust trolleys ending up with broken wheels while walking through rainy Basel (recent memory) or Glasgow (almost forgotten), or find it with a broken wheel at the baggage reclaim. Two trolleys and carry-on luggage are a pain in subways, but I must take them, as I cannot afford taxis.

Anyway: I started ordering the North Face trolley with my phone. At the end of the order, everything

seemed to scramble, so I opened my laptop and started all over again, filling in VAT numbers, invoice and delivery address and supplying all unavoidable data that eventually make our (digital) life so speedy these day's – especially after researching various price-comparing search-engines. Once I managed to purchase the trolley, I continued doing some administration, booking invoices on the online management system we use. It was then that I noticed I had paid twice for the same trolley with inline-skate-wheels. I called the company, who had not yet registered my first payment, but told me they would correct it.
And indeed, within the next hour a cancellation email popped up. The next day, one hour after the scheduled delivery, the delivery guy – who I know, as he always delivers packages of the neighbour across the street who are apparently never at home, came to bring only one trolley, well wrapped in plastic that was, on its turn, well wrapped in a big cardboard box.'

What this says to me, is that our independent publishing culture rests upon reduction of costs largely achieved by the sacrifices and efforts of individuals that operate these imprints and activities. Publishers like myself can avoid the ethical pain or calamity of operating a more mainstream publishing business defensively believing that they are circulating content they believe in; however, this does come at a personal sacrifice – including limiting time for other capital making activities.

<u>Integrity and the economy of actors</u>

A more recent finding of a 'market' meant that self-publishing developed into a more formalised structure like that of traditional or larger publishing houses. This meant that the publisher would employ or manage multiple players in the field and the various aspects of the production, from editing, to design and dealing with printers, print specs and distribution partnerships. This management of more players ultimately means that an independent publisher's early idealistic DIY freedoms, specifically, the objectives and approach, changed hands to one from independence to that of one distributed to many actors or parties. The positive outcomes of such changes meant that, with more distribution and more resources, print runs could increase, therefore reducing the costs per book unit and subsequently turning a profit on some titles if it sold enough. This profit becomes useful, in order to fund future projects or support a community of practice. A more negative outcome is the more people that are involved in a production, there is an increasing hierarchy and bureaucracy to be managed; the costs for this labour is often unaccounted for.

Therefore, following this increased profit, myself and

colleagues became much more aware of labour needed and the labour conditions required to enable this distribution. Onomatopee for instance, began to produce many books with small printers in Eastern Europe where the printing estimates were much reduced to printers in Western European countries – we found cheaper and cheaper ways of producing books using these networks and contacts. At the same time, due to high labour costs in Western Europe, we bought a shrink-wrapping machine in order to shrink-wrap books ourselves to further save costs. As example, we are currently paying twenty-one thousand euro for the printing of a forthcoming title but we will shrink wrap the publication ourselves to save 800 euro. This is the reality of the opportunities that global distribution presents and a real issue of progressive cultural production. Our early entrepreneurial aspirations, to remain independent, DIY and engaged now seems naïve; we did not know how to take on the responsibility of the serious cultural engagement you have as publisher.

Yet, this engagement clouded our ethical judgement and all too easily pushed for free labour. I still believe this is a sad reality, regardless of the suffering it produces, that many cultural producers will still benefit from free or low-cost labour practices. For Onomatopee this meant that the publisher is not paid for their in-kind but also now expert labour such as editorial advice, production support etc, while the graphic designers, authors and text editors, who were needed to produce the basic, raw result, do receive payment.

The mission of producing an alternative by bringing these types of smaller niche art projects and art writing into wider circulation cannot primarily be for financial gain, rather it is to share ideas and texts that may sit outside of the mainstream or classic notion of cultural capital. This should be the objective to garner public support of such publications – that these publishers are serving a gap in the market, to avoid insular culture being reproduced. Public support or funding for such publications enables more people to be paid for their labour and to in turn expand the reach of progressive cultural pursuits and repress the scope of 'uncommon' conditions in bookmaking.

Authors are essential players in the ecology of cultural publishing who elevate the scope of a project and provide the project with its urgency and legitimacy, authors coupled with a well-founded narration and framing by a skilled editor makes for a solid publication. In saying this, cultural publishing is not academic publishing, and therefore has a freedom to employ various styles and forms of writing such as poetic, philosophical, essayist, columnist and so forth. What therefore matters in the case of independent social engaged publishing, is to publish lesser known – or more risk-taking authors and art writing.

Independent publishers have an opportunity to platform lesser-known and more marginalised art writers, artists, designers, typographers and content producers, or even host other initiatives to offer these a wider reach. The result of a quality funded production, or gesture (in my opinion), should reflect the participatory capacity of the production of those that have engaged in its production.

In closing

Where art publishing, by tradition, prompts established power, progressive cultural publishing is the art worker's cultural equal in publishing. As independent books are slowly finding their way towards a wider audience, the market will change from these stocked in international selected independent bookstores to bigger chain stores. I hope to see wider audiences slowly familiarising themselves with different art writing and voices beyond the very much cherished few we find at international fairs, and distributors willing to supporting this diversification, and booksellers willing to endorse such activities.

Of course, the books made by Onomatopee, cannot cater to everyone and evidently many of our books are exclusive in their support of the marginal. Yet, increasing these books do reach audiences farther afield. Consumers, interested producers, funding bodies, cultural producers and everyone engaged in this economy should become aware of the opportunities of progressive cultural publishing, and we should continue to organise together... we cannot leave this to commercial galleries or private museums. The public sector by nature, cannot be up to date with progressive public interest. In 'progressive cultural publishing' there might not be much money, but it has developed an infrastructure that provides opportunity to influence culture more widely and a supportive community of practice for a generation of art writers.

I feel that life finds quality when we face struggles and culture is the place where we should and can explore life the most.

Peace, love and regulated chaos.

Producing the contemporary along the hegemony of a past-day elite and a present silent majority - A 2016 perspective on independent art spaces in the Netherlands

(text as published in 2016)

Over the past decade, I've been given quite a number of books by artist- run and independent art spaces, published on the occasion of their X-year existence, meant as calls-to-authority to policy makers and as relation gifts to the network. Hardly ever do matters reach another level: that of collective organisation, exchange of knowledge and so forth. People are simply happy celebrating yet another X-years of existence. It's also for this financial and time-wise lack to go beyond, that this text will not turn out a thought-through analysis of the Dutch situation, of contrasts between regions and nations, continents and cultures, but rather a kind or oral impression of the Dutch side – possibly the Noord-Brabant provincial side – that is to say my side of the story... for whatever that might be worth.

I came to work in the 'independent' arts in 2003 as a curator working for the artist-run space Lokaal 01, at the time based in Breda (NL) and Antwerp (BE). No idea why they hired me: I was just a bit of a 'want-to-figure-himself-out' kid, still studying arts and science at the University (not even an artist), who only just before, via artist friends, came about some art spaces, somewhere off centre in nearby cities. The people who ran it started it back in the late '70s–early '80s or came in after studying at art school and having started a career in the arts. Even though I was a bit of a strange duck to the organisation, I learned pretty much all I needed to know to work in the arts at Lokaal 01 – even more than at the university where I graduated a little later in arts policy (a particular history proven worthless to me while producing the future and having to cope with the day-to-day blindness of cultural policy's prophecies) and cultural identity (good) – and even more working at the Van Abbemuseum some years later, where learning about the arts was more about familiarising myself with forms of meetings.

What I learned at Lokaal 01, a knock-out for me at the time, is that there are certain people who go about discovering really particular stuff by their own conditions, not so much through conceptual written analysis (philosophy), or by test and check and double-check (natural sciences), or fiction (literature), but rather by creating experiences that through matter enter our environment and our sociability, and thus become present. These people (many call them artists) were to be respected, for who is a specialist in that particular unknown but that person, and how better to respect that experimental domain than by respecting the integrity of that person, and how better to position and promote that domain than by using the only way to manifest it besides the encounter of the work (which is the responsibility of the artist): by using ugly words?

In love with speculative wonder, I suddenly felt I had found my place. This bunch of inarticulate individuals offered me a home.

–

The 1970s and early 1980s was a time when the economy went down while the welfare state was establishing itself, under guidance of the typical Dutch compartmentalisation of society through top-down political governance, wherein all Catholics and Protestants, the Socialists and the – at the time minor – Liberals, submitted to the few political parties who ran the nation together. In the enduring, yet slowly dying, spirit of a post-war urge to stimulate cultural uplifting, the late 80s and early 90s became a time wherein any graduate self-proclaimed artist could get a minimum wage, and when huge collections of public art were gathered, consisting of all too many locally produced works (many of which were recently dumped on the market or just put out with the trash). Even up to 2012, there was additional support in income for recent art school graduates. This was all inspired by notions of cultural capital, dominant within high-culture, when people visiting operas experienced historical legacies of revolutions after they drove in with leased cars, and after having purchased an artwork in a gallery, not knowing they were not part of society but were only part of a ruling class.
As a consequence of this top-down imposed idea of cultural uplifting (possibly a secret fear for radicalisa-

tion among smart dissidents to society), a minor part of policy made it all too easy for a complete social group of societal drop-outs called artists to give rise to their own economies in artist-run spaces. Their position was informed by motives such as (in our city) "inherent quality of arts" (I never knew what that motive meant) or, as (in our province), the "autonomous visual qualities of arts" (never knew what that meant either). Primarily these motives were the all-too-generic rules to fixate an art policy that supported the idea of emancipation through cultural uplifting. This bureaucratisation of bullshit motives turned out to be the gospel of a self-centred art world developed in parallel to the rise of the '80s yuppie culture of self-enriching kids that slowly, but gradually, took over the cultural authority of the post-war baby-boom generation; that of former hippies who effectively ended up being complete social democratic revisionists, too tolerant to see through the decadence of the third way.

—

Over the course of the mid-'90s and into the early 2000s the Dutch art field slowly – very slowly in hindsight – started to change (no paradigm shift, simply little improvements). Pushed by the Mondriaan Foundation (founded in 1994), art spaces and artist-run spaces had to 'professionalise', and as their role shifted to mediation, the name label slowly changed to 'presentation spaces'. Artistically this meant that curating entered the field, and in managing terms it meant that policy became a more prominent factor in day-to-day management of these spaces.

These changes were – and still are – considered a doom- scenario to those celebrating unconditional artistic autonomy (inherent value/autonomous qualities) within the art field itself. On the opposite end, even though there was a slowly growing awareness amongst policy makers that things should not to be taken for granted anymore, they did sustain a scene of independent art spaces. This proceeded for a while, as the former hegemonic political parties kept ruling the nation, even though the Catholic middle-of-the-road block lost position over the course of the 1990s.
But then something started to change, as in the early 2000s pioneering Dutch populist Pim Fortuyn stood up and the nation polarised, and polarised even more when a mentally troubled guy gunned him down.
In hindsight Fortuyn seems the ideal Dutch citizen: outspoken, humanist, indifferent to authority yet tolerant to difference. What really changed was the turn to complete economic liberalism wherein the liberal idea of cultural uplifting stopped being a top-down public responsibility; while for Fortuyn, solidarity and cultural uplifting were apparent even if on an individual basis, this stopped being evident to his even more radical populist followers, resulting in a comple-

te abandonment of respect for liberal research and development – formerly perceived as Cultural Capital – and instead opting for individual choice within capitalism under cultural protectionism inspired by a fear of the different. Over the course of the late 2000s, this idea completely put aside the cheap rhetoric of former-yuppie baby-boomers, rejecting the idea that public funding serves cultural uplift, that culture and arts has inherent quality, that there is something such as autonomous visual qualities. This is the point when government policy changed motivation: when belief for non-economic motivated research development and experiences were set apart by its prime investor. The objective turned to economic results, to independent, self-organised turnover, primarily via social segregation of target groups that divide culture among likes and un-likes. Although the arts, academic research and much alike, might have segregated from egalitarian access, it was primarily because mediation was supported too little in a society that simply did not respect cultural capital anymore, and turned to experiences. The citizen became a consumer and a producer. No greater cause in the arts is possible anymore, as the greater objective is no longer supported.

—

When, as a result of this change of perception, the arts were faced in early 2013 with their biggest budget cuts ever, they completely lost track of progressive public

interest and had to turn to segregation even more, whether it be a focus for a segregated public fund to have blind people visit a museum of visual arts; or a focus for a segregated public by making profit via a party for youngsters during a museum night;
or a focus for a segregated public with a high-end entrance fee to an afternoon with collectors. It is all market motivated and audiences will never blend anymore: the institutions will just change the interior, clothes and tongue to meet the demographics of their visiting consumers. But what this means most of all is that the perception of art will always be framed to the eye of the target group, and, as a result of this turn to the target group over the former humanist focus for cultural elevation, the economic basis for independent production for a greater cause of humanist man is abandoned. From now on, art will align itself with an agenda, with a subculture, with a segregated economy. There is no public good, there will only be publics of which some might survive and some might be ignored as unviable.
The problem within resultant contemporary cultural consumerism is the lack of what's on offer, of access to ambiguity and doubt and of radical differences produced from a position standing above the cultural spectrum (as art effectively should). This leaves an inability to face the contemporary: to actively engage the doubtfulness of our being in the face of our history, and in facing our (lack of) opportunities. The idea

that art is about joy and beauty f**ks up the capacity of art as a force of cultural empowerment and is a mindless capitalist construct exploiting a capitalist experience economy. Basically, this is a political choice, as we can also opt for other options.

I feel that it is out of a necessity to speak up for this humanist solidarity that independent spaces exist, stimulate production of a cultural meta- individual uniqueness, and try to deliver that with all the means available to an audience. It is for this reason, I feel, that Dutch independent spaces still call themselves presentation spaces – ranging from small spaces in the provinces such as Hedah in Maastricht, to established places such as Witte de With in Rotterdam – and have organised themselves in a union called De Zaak Nu (The Now Case), which is the equivalent of Common Practice in the UK. Likewise we see a new awareness among Dutch artists who organised themselves in Platform BK: a new collective way of organising work-spaces for art, design and architecture in ceramics, metal, graphics and more; and see growing awareness within a relatively a new type of organisation: art-clusters who rent out spaces, manage studio spaces and more. This is happening at various geopolitical levels: the city, the region and national.
I know many of my colleagues in the field will disagree, but for a long time, prior to the excessive budget cuts that forged a cultural paradigm shift, the

art field, and the independent spaces in particular, felt they were tolerant to culture while they actually turned their backs to culture. Nevertheless the accomplishments within this all-too- segregated scene were remarkable in the way that it progressed our legacy of humanism into an era of increasing complexity. We need to be able to doubt within our horizontal proximity, and art does so within our experience, within direct encounters. It does so by demanding us to experience by our human capacity, positioned above taste, religion or anything whatsoever, and thus liberal in that sense. That is the biggest task for independent contemporary art spaces. It will never be unconditional or autonomous, even when the conditions might be vague, too experimental to legitimise in parallel to the experience of the work delivered, but that is exactly what living in the contemporary means. That is what true cultural production, true development means: setting hearts and minds, opening up. This implies the belief that we can all think for ourselves, and the necessity of battle while facing our present reality. It's a way to counter fear for eternal cultural shifts. As any other hegemonic culture we call democracy, it might be said that The Netherlands is simply changing one form of cultural dictatorship (that of an elite) for another (that of the silent majority, unwilling to emancipate). Yet what is most problematic is the fact that we ignore the use of the human capacity our parents have left to us as well. Why should we not finish the project of modernity, called emancipation and freedom, especially as hierarchy is abandoned and the individual is finally left on its own?

I'm active in local lobbying for small art spaces (K9 in Eindhoven), initiated provincial organisation, and am a board member of De Zaak Nu. It's a f***ing lot of volunteering work but together we can gain knowledge that helps us to inform others and ourselves. This knowledge can inform all stakeholders, either private or public, and convince them to invest. Locally we're too few spaces to come up with serious data, but nationally we can – and this data can be mirrored in a local setting and therefore be of representative value. Moreover, within the local scale, some organisations are featured who don't have paid staff (permanent or freelance), and might not even have a permanent office, and are therefore in a very precarious situation, while within the national context, some big organisations are featured. What I mean to say is that we should not be afraid of other levels, but should try and push for the right attitude in all levels. Whom if not us should do this? Nobody is going to care otherwise.

And if that would not work out, we can always turn to revolution, I once heard Rebecca Gordon-Nesbitt say. I would not dare to argue that.

End to humility?

(by means of conclusion)

Progressive cultural production is a caring struggle. Now that the neoliberal leash that kept us alive is dissolving at an increasing rate,, we could feel victimized and outcast. In this environment it can be tempting to express ourselves in desperation, which might widen the gap with those living another paradigm, and create a more violent atmosphere. We do not have to follow the aggression of the ignorant and should not be provoked. If we turn to ourselves, be ignorant to decadence, endure the gap we experience and accept a more precarious lifestyle, we could provide an alternative response, grounded in care. Such a position will demand us to balance our needs. It will be difficult to judge.

We expressed humility to neoliberal cultures in how we spoke out and were not to humble ourselves while doing it. We need to switch this around: speak out of a caring position and simultaneously become more resilient in humbleness to ourselves. We are likely to fail ourselves and others on this path, as the hegemonic cultural economy at large is so destructive, but we should never let go of investing trust in the grim gray of the culture we care about and live in.

Colophon

Set Margins' #50

Care where no-one does

A grassroots style guide to progressive cultural production, anticipating neoliberal to national conservative times..

ISBN: 978-90-834041-5-8

Written and designed by Freek Lomme
Text editors: my sister Kaatje, who lives in the UK, checked all aside of the previousley published texts.
Printer: Printon, Tallin (Est.)
Fonts: Tonka by Celine Hurka, Lao MN and Adorno Noveau by Salvador Rodriguez Diego Aravena.

Made possible thanks to:
I paid this myself. Hope I'll get the print of about 2.500 euro + the material costs of publishing (1500 or so for storage, transport, photography etc.) returned.

First edition, 2024
www.setmargins.press

These texts have previousley been published:

Fashion victims and social fabrics
in:
Copy Nature: elementary sentiments (2011).
Ellen Zoete and Freek Lomme (Eds.). Onomatopee.

The truth is "out there" - Stakes and responsibilities of rhetoric's within contemporary culture's design realm
in:
Culture, innovation and the economy (2018) Biljana Mickov and James E. Doyle (Eds.). Routledge.

Balancing ethics and economies: A push for a new perspective on art publishing
in:
Art Writing in Crisis (2021). Brad Haylock and Megan Patty (Eds.). Sternberg Press.

Producing the contemporary along the hegemony of a past-day elite and a present silent majority - A 2016 perspective on independent art spaces in the Netherlands
in:
Artist-Run Europe (2016). Gavin Murphy and Mark Cullen (Eds.). First print via Onomatopee, second print via Set Margins' (2024)